The Eyes of HER Heart and Soul

Ta'Korya Gist

BookLeaf Publishing

India | USA | UK

This is dedicated to anyone who reads it.
May it make you think, stir your heart,
bring joy to your soul and help make you
whole.

ACKNOWLEDGEMENT

I thank the one person that made me understand that I was different and my differences are what made me indescribable and great.

Thank You.
-TK

PREFACE

No Doubt In Victory.

A Walk around the corner,
Can be as easy as the thought.
Why is doubt in your mind?
Why doubt what you sought out?
Take the journey you face as a challenge for
victory.

Encapsulated I

Encapsulate yourself like a caterpillar in a
cocoon.
Be the embodiment of strength, courage,
and dignity,
The embodiment of beauty within,
A virtuous woman you will find.
And then come shine bright,
Pure Love, Pure Light and Beautiful like a
Butterfly.

Encapsulated II

Encapsulated like a caterpillar in a cocoon,
I Arise, woken, strong enough to spread my
wings to break the resistance of these walls,
This comfortable familiarity of life.
I Arise as someone new doing new things,
and live life once more.
-A Butterfly

Behold!

She is the epitome of a Woman behold!
She loves deeper than the ocean below.
Her mind is of many clouds, the shapes and
heights she can go.
And she's so grounded she seeded your
soul.
Her ancestors gave birth to a nation that
doesn't treat her as the whole.
You cannot define her,
A original and she knows.
She caters to your heart and on the stove.
So well rounded and a silhouette of indigo
Down right rider for the man she shows,
That she's a well fit mother for the child she
helps bloom and grow
Sorry no bets behold!
She is more precious than rubies; she
cannot be sold.

The Love is real. The love is not.

5

You say you don't steal,
But you stole my heart, was that real?
Or is it a lie like you pretending something is
real when it is not?
A common misdemeanor or is it federally
illegal and detrimental from the start?
Meeting someone that'll support your
decisions and love you from the bottom of
their heart,
Will have my heart stop, or skip a beat, and
drop.
But is it real?
All I can say is people don't come with
warning labels from the crib.

Trauma and Scars

My Heart ripped open,
Then heals.
The scars made me stronger,
But built a wall up on a hill.

The Truth

Telling the truth
But you won't believe me
Ridin' coast to cost and back
And you still don't see me
Spoke to you
and waited for hours
For a call back I never got back
I was sour
I guess it's a game to you because
You know I got that power
And it's so strange to you
I like to cope in the shower
But it's a shame that you are
Scared of this flower
Eye create more than beauty
Eye, Myself, I'll blossom...
but every time I give you gold nuggets
You will toss them.
Finding foe concepts of the truth
But if there's love there why would I
Try to hurt you
Back then I was fighting for the truth
It really hurt when I would get nothing
Because I loved you.
You inspire me to challenge myself
And strive for the clouds

We are like the sun and the moon,
they have times they sit out,
and let the other shine,
no scream no shout,
But without a doubt,
The only one that has lied
Is you.
With the truth you
You would not let out

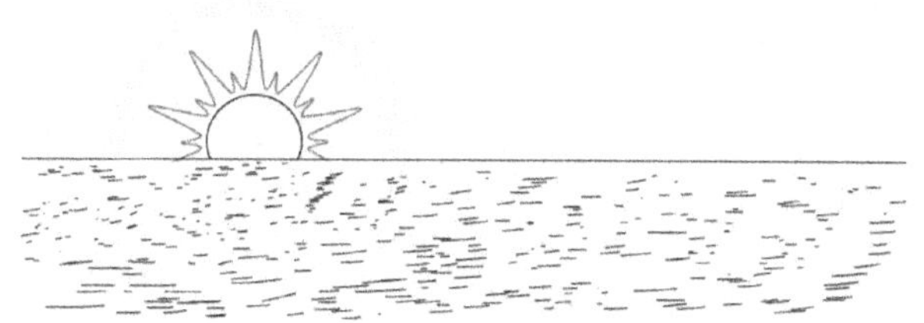

I Am

They say you don't need the flashy and the
extra,
but look at me,
I am flashy,
I am extra.
I am over the top,
but I am also simple,
and it's easy to be beautiful and natural.
I am flawless,
I am phenomenal,
I am glamorous.
Also royalty.
And my authority in my morality,
Will have you seeing my reality.
And loving me?
My creativity goes beyond the clouds so far;
Uncertainty Is Guaranteed.

All that is

All Pure; that she is.
She's spiritual too
Closed eyes ponder why that is.
Maybe because she was respected as she
is.
She was connected with a man and loved
by a king.
A god loved a goddess that is.
Teachings by he and understandings by
she.
The sun and the moon that is.
The gaze left with stars
The Bright light that she is
The light that shines between them;
will always turn heads.
A King and a Queen that is.

Alone or Together?

A King with no queen

is like coffee with no creamer,

eye shadows with no shimmer.

light bulbs and no dimmer,

and Calls with no ringer;

They can stand alone but they are better
together.

Covered

Even though this flower was picked by its stem it never dies as it preserves in this resin.

The Valley Path

Deep in the valley, darkness lives there.

Don't give in, and don't have fear.

Don't lose focus, and don't shed tears.

Shine bright like the light of heaven is there.

Keep your weapon; your mind, sharp like a
spear,

So you can move your mountains till all your
paths are clear.

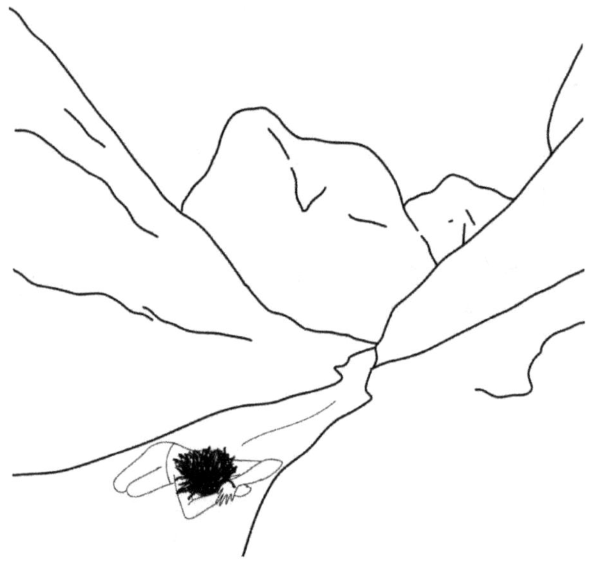

No Doubt in Victory

A walk around the corner
Can be as easy as the thought.
Why is doubt in your mind?
Why doubt what you sought out?
Take the journey you face as a challenge for
victory.

KING

Black king; brown King you have come so
far.
To be a leading example of revolutionary
change you've raised the bar.
As you identify the faults of this country you
remember the origin of each scar.
Pure light, Pure love, that's what you are.
With your power I'm proud that many black
men don't stand in sorrow.
Hope for change welcomes tomorrow.
Black king; black queen wishes to stand
with you and fight. There's strength in
numbers and awakening sight.
Until then we will fight together in spirit to do
what's right.

Affirm

Today is anew, and I love you.
You have beat challenges and trials that
tried to break you.
Did not let any bad overtake you.
Let the positive vibes awaken you.
You are doing a great job
I have faith in you.
You will meet every goal
I am hopeful too
That everything you do turns golden just like
you.
And that love will multiply and be attracted
back to you.

Blacks

Black people are not a fashion statement
Brown people are not a trend.
We are who we say we are.
Kings and Queens just to begin.
My people are not a trend.
We are skilled and we will ascend
We are who we say we are.
We are in the beginning and at the end.

Relations

Be confident in how you feel about them,
but don't rush, take your time,
don't be just romantic,
be intuitive and love their mind.

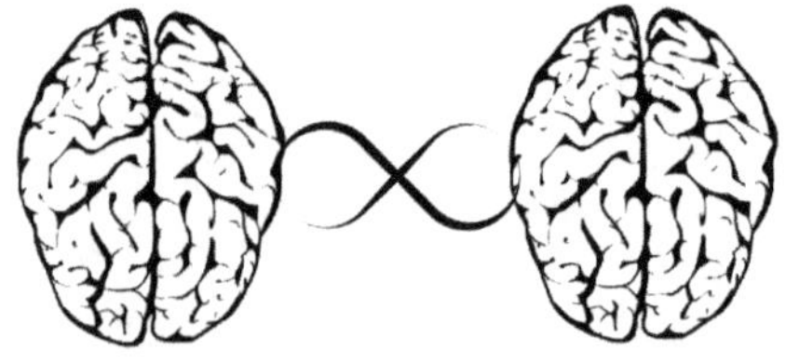

Love Letter

25

I want to love past your traumas.
I want to add to your Nirvana.
In perfect peace no added drama.
I didn't take all this time to grieve
over the best option for me,
it took me growing up from 2016,
To realize you'll always be right for me.
I don't want anything,
but to make you happier babe,
secure a life with you,
Show love, be real, stay true,
and maybe if I leave Just Enough Clues;
You will understand the symbols tattooed,
 in the middle of my chest for you.

Yours,
TK

KaMari

27

Her sweet laugh, and goofy cute smile,
high spirits, and energy has her going for
miles.
Her green eyes and light skin just glows.
When I see her the smartest Princess I
know.
She is my blessing that keeps me on my
toes.
Everything in me wants to give her the best.
So I work diligently like the 1% not like the
rest.
And if I can do one thing to impact her life, I
would explain our culture and make sure
she knows her rights.
Create generational wealth by great
grandchildren we won't lose sight.
Of why we love, do good and why I taught
her to fight.

They Hate

They hate that I'm beautiful,
They hate that I'm smart,
They hate that I'm a realist,
They hate when I'm right,
What they see,
They don't have in life,
And all the jealous energy
Is a self mental fight,
Some just don't understand
Pure Love,
Pure Light.

The Odyssey

Take me on a journey of beauty and power.
Flowers blooming up under the sun for
hours. Beauty only happens overnight in the
Odyssey.
Locs & Hair, Twisted and braided up so
tightly.
Silver stacked Bob was it for me.
Diamonds shining in my hair oh so icy
Seeing all the pieces come together, so
exciting.
Show Time! Let me explain why I'm writing.
The first on the runway stirred up the fire
inside me.
Head up!
Walk Strong!
Like a Goddess is the policy.
Walked around like a Queen.
So Righteously.
So glad I was a part of the Exotic Hair
Odyssey.

Warrior Queen

32

Some say it's something about me that's so
mysterious.
Truth is I'm the light that shines in darkness.
There's no weakness in my uniqueness.
But this is me. I feel like this everyday.
Strong in my beliefs.
Stand firm in my Authority.
Bold and Beautiful and loved by majority.
A natural born leader, independent and
individuality.
Ambitious, living consistently with my
originality.
Day and Night I strive to connect the Seen
with the Unseen.
I am an explorer and an innovator.
I see the horizon and where the promise
leads.
With my soft and warm exterior.
Many perceive me as a gentle, safe harbor.
But I conquer as a Black woman,
As a Queen,
As a mother.
I am a Warrior.

9 789357 446587